Lord of The Sabbath 10-3-16 interior size 5.5x8.5
All scriptures not given in the text are written out in the appendix.
Appendix #1 large portions of Scriptures- p17-47
Appendix #2 small portions of Scriptures- p47-50
Index (reference) p56 **Summary** p50-56
Bible Scriptures using the word Sabbath p62-65

[1] When Jesus terminated His 40 days in the wilderness, **Matt. 4:1-11** p40, [D] He went into the land of the Gentiles to fulfill the prophecy of Isaiah in the Old Testament. See **Matt 4:13-16**. P40 [D]

[2] The prophecy was the Salvation of the Gentiles. **Matt. 4:14-17** p40 Jesus returned to Galilee preaching two things: First: repentance and second follow me. **Matt. 4:17-19** p40 But Jesus gave His disciples a command not to go to the gentiles. **Matt. 10:5** p47 But Jesus said that He wouldn't either. **Matt.15: 22-24**. p47

[3] For three years Jesus went to only the lost sheep of Israel and then was killed. So what happened to the prophecy that the Gentiles would be saved. It would happen but not by Jesus, until after the ascension. It was by the Holy Spirit by Paul

[4] Getting back to what Jesus taught; repentance and Following Him. Everything Jesus said and did in His three years of ministry is hinged on these two things: Repent for the Kingdom of God is at hand and follow me and I will make you fishers of men. Neither one of these commandments are onetime events. Salvation starts with forgiveness and we grow by continuing to forgive others throughout our

Christian life. Second, to be fishers of men we must first have someone show us discipleship. Then the process continues so that everyone will be teaching discipleship. Even in marriage the man is to teach his family discipleship.

[5] We always have a need to ask for forgiveness from the time we are saved to the time we go to heaven. And being more like Jesus is discipleship. Both pertains to ourselves and others. We need to continue to discipline ourselves by having at least one disciple under us at all times.

[6] Discipleship is the key to Christianity. Jesus did it all through his ministry. He couldn't be stopped until they killed Him. But he had to die so he would send the Holy Spirit to live in us to be like Jesus, in word and action. The suffering of Jesus dying on the cross reflects on us, dying to self. "For if we have been united together in the likeness of His death we shall be also in the likeness of His resurrection." **Romans 6:5** p48

[7] Ananias came to Paul with a message from Jesus that Paul was called to the Gentiles. Paul obeyed that calling and since that time he received persecution from the Jews as Jesus did. He also died from the hands of the Jews as Jesus did. **Acts 9:15** p48 Since Paul was called to the Gentiles, God inspired him to write instructions to the Gentiles which was the book of Romans. Scholars call Romans a book of doctrine but Jesus called His doctrine to do the will of His Father. And then Jesus said that if you love me, keep my commandments.

Paul used the word doctrine only twice in the book of Romans. In the Gospels several time Jesus said to be careful of the doctrine of man. The Commandments Jesus gave to the Jews are for the Gentiles also but He also inspired Paul to give clarity to His commandments. So the Book of Romans is very important to understand the commandments of Christ.

[8] The word doctrine is use twice 1. **Romans 16:17** p57 where the emphasis on doctrine concerns causing division. 2. **Romans 6:17** p57

[9] Doctrine and commands are not the same things. Doctrine explains the scriptures and commandments are Scriptures to obey. It is better to obey than to sacrifice, even if the sacrifice is your own life. **1 Corinthians 13:3.** The word commandment is found 8 times in the Book of **Romans 7:8-13 13:9 & 16:26. See index** p57-58

[10] Doctrine has been a big issue in argumentation and caused church division and killings since the beginning of Christianity. Examples are between the: Christians and the Jews, the Catholic and the Orthodox, the Catholic and the Lutheran church, and not to mention the over 20,000 doctrinal forms of denominational churches and cults up to the present time, having conflicts.

[11] Over 70 million Christians lost their life over doctrinal issues or persecution since Christ's first coming. In many cases doctrine and commandment can mean the same thing but the commandments of the Old Testament determined obedience to the

law. The New Testament is established by the commands of Jesus. You find about 50 of them in the Gospels and they also are to be obeyed. In the Old Testament there are 613 Laws to obey. There is one commandment Jesus puts above all the others and that is to love God and others. In fact Jesus says that all the other commandments are hinged on the command to love which is call the Great Commandment.

[12] Jesus came only to the Jewish people and love them until He was betrayed by one of His own disciples which Jesus loved unto the end. And it wasn't Jesus that put an end to Judas' life. Jesus loved him to much even to think of doing him harm. When Paul was given leadership over the Gentiles He was permitted to change some of the commandments between the Old dispensation of law to the dispensation under grace. These are all the facts as I see them, because doctrine seemingly is here to stay.

[13] On the most part Doctrine would be the interpretation of Scripture. And Commandments would be Application of Scripture. Children are expected to obey their parents. The Lord wants obedient people. We are under only one basic command and that is to love others the way Jesus loves us. Love out-weighs the love of the world by loving them that don't love you. The sermon of the mount tells us what that means many times.
Matthew 5:10-13: 5:21-22; 5:27-28; 5:38-39-41; 5:43-44. See appendix #2. P48-49

[14] Luke was the only Gentile writer in the New Testament. He followed Paul and gave the story of his trip to Rome in the book of Acts. Paul had Persecution when he included the Gentiles as being equal to the Jew in God's sight. From that time the Jew and the Gentile have not worked together. After that the Gentiles continued Christianity and the Jews were rejected through their own action of putting Christ on the cross and started to kill Christians in large numbers.

[15] In the last days the Jews will be re-commissioned. Many scholars believe at the end times the Jews and the Gentiles will work together. But in **Revelation 18:4** p58 see index[58] The sin of the Gentile church reached heaven and the true believers were told to leave the church. The Church doesn't have a second best to fall back on. I believe that the Jew took over the church as prophesied and the Gentiles that remained righteous were under the Jewish leadership. Many scholars believe that the rapture will happen before the Jews are recommissioned. I believe that there will be only one second coming of Christ which will have incorporate the rapture with the second coming of Christ.

[16] Scriptures do seem to indicate several raptures but it may mean important events are repeated several times to make it a major emphasis. There is a separate judgement for the lost and the save but one second coming of Christ.

[17] In **Acts chapter 10** pg. 44 Peter had to have a vision to kill and eat unclean animals. That met changes were to take place. Not only for salvation for the Gentiles but also a change in the Sabbath day regulations.

[18] Paul was willing to bear much suffering so I believe that he was able to have a deeper understanding of Christ. **Acts 9:4** "Then Paul fell to the ground and heard a voice saying to him. Saul. Saul why are you persecuting Me?" This was far from the only time Paul had to suffer for the Lord Jesus.

[19] There is a tie-in between Going to the Gentiles with the Gospel and the Sabbath day worship. The unclean animals that Peter had in his vision seemingly now is permissible for the Gentiles to eat. **Acts 10** p44-47 Peter hesitated about wanting the Gentile to become Jewish which kept tension between the Jews and the Gentiles.

[20] So going to the Gentile gave Paul insights on how to regulate the Holy days. The Sabbath had strict regulations and to break any of them had the death penalty. The Book of Romans is a doctrinal book written to the Gentiles.

[21] Since Jesus said he was the Lord of the Sabbath; it put the New Testament regulations under the authority of Paul. And this has been accepted by Christianity when the Book of Romans was canonized in the year 375 AD. Roman doctrine wasn't directly what Jesus said, but Jesus giving

Paul the approval by Paul's own writing which became inspired by God.

[22] The first 100,000 Christian converts were mostly all Jews. Jesus was a Jew and wanted the Jewish Nation to come into the dispensation of Grace. But through there rebellion having rejected Jesus, being responsible for His death, the Jews were rejected by Jesus.

[23] Because Paul went to the Gentiles, he also changed many of the hard rules of the Sabbath. There were about 1,500 Sabbath Day rules. By the book of Romans that was changed. The Epistle could have been called the Gospel according to Paul because it was filled with the doctrine of Jesus, even though Paul was not one of the original twelve disciples. All 1,500 rules are not in the Bible because the priests were allow to add new rules when conditions arose down through the years. So we do not know what they are. For example: the law that you can't heal on the Sabbath is not in the Bible yet they told Jesus it was a Sabbath rule. But Jesus changed that quickly by saying that He was the Lord of the Sabbath.

[24] Jesus said, "The Sabbath was made for man". It is like saying a man was not made for a car but the car was made for men, which means that man came first and the car was invented to serve man. **Matthew 2:27-28**. "The Sabbath was made for man and not man for the Sabbath: Therefore the Son of

Man is Lord also of the Sabbath." This means Jesus has set new rules for the Sabbath.

[25] Note in **Romans 14** p42 Paul talks about all the conditions of the Sabbath Day but now in the New Testament they are called the Holy days. There is no restriction to which day or days and what food to eat. It is up to each man in his own mind but the restriction is not to judge others if they have different views on the Holy days or what to eat.

[26] Sabbath Day laws were included in our civil law for about 150 years. I can remember in the 1940's all stores had to be closed on Sunday and no professional sports could be played on Sunday. They were called the 'Blue Laws.'

[27] When our country was formed in 1776 all government employee's had to have a good standing in a local church and they brought their Bibles to congress because all laws had to be backed up with Scriptures. This went on until the mid-1900's. When Christians stopped daily discipline, forced discipline from the government started to take over.

[28] Now every organization in our country sees the fallibility of human nature and uses discipline without love to force the rules of man upon everyone. Even if a person is not a leader we like to tell others they are wrong. That can cause fights and marriages are no exceptions. This is the same reason why two nations will go to war.

[29] The discipline that the fruit of the Spirit God refers to in **Galatians 5:22-23** is: The fruit of the spirit is: love, joy peace, patience, gentleness, goodness, faith, meekness and temperance which means self-control.

[30] If we do not control ourselves as Christians others will do it for us. **1 Corinthians 11** the chapter on the Lord's Supper, it says in verse **11:31** "For if we would judge ourselves, we would not be judged." Judging comes when Christians do not have self-discipline.

Notice that the fruit of the spirit is in the singular. The noun 'fruit' is singular and the verb 'is' are both singular. Then it mentions the nine fruits of the Spirit. This means you cannot have one without the others. The first is love and the last is self-control. There is no love without self-control. The same is true for all of the fruits.

[31] The meaning of the Sabbath (in my mind) is: if I follow Christ's commands I would not be under Old Testament law. That means to deny self which is (temperance) & be willing to suffer when I think I am right.

[32] When Jesus finished his 40 days in the wilderness He went into the land of the Gentiles to fulfil a prophecy from The Old Testament.

[33] **Matthew 4:11-22** "v11Then the devil leaveth him, and, behold, angels came and ministered unto him. v12 Now when Jesus had heard that John was cast into prison, he departed into Galilee; v13 And leaving Nazareth, he came and dwelt in

Capernaum, which is upon the sea coast, in the borders of Zabulon and Nephthalim: v14 That it might be fulfilled which was spoken by Esaias the prophet, saying, v15 The land of Zabulon, and the land of Nephthalim, *by* the way of the sea, beyond Jordan, Galilee of the Gentiles; v16 The people which sat in darkness saw great light; and to them which sat in the region and shadow of death, light is sprung up. v17 From that time Jesus began to preach, and to say, <u>Repent: for the kingdom of heaven is at hand.</u> v18 And Jesus, walking by the sea of Galilee, saw two brethren, Simon called Peter, and Andrew his brother, casting a net into the sea: for they were fishers. v19 And he said unto them, <u>Follow me, and I will make you fishers of men</u>. v20 And they straightway left *their* nets, and followed him. 21 And going on from there, he saw other two brethren, James *the son* of Zebedee, and John his brother, in a ship with Zebedee their father, mending their nets; and he called them. v22 And they immediately left the ship and their father, and followed him."

[34] Here are the situations I had to understand according to Matthew 4:11-22 (above)

(1) To resist temptation I will go through suffering so great that angels would have to minister to me.

(2) Why did Jesus go to the Gentiles yet His three years of ministry was only to the lost sheep of Israel. Matthew 4:15-16 (above).

(3) Why were the first words of Jesus: <u>repent</u> and <u>follow me,</u> so important. See the above underlined portions in Matthew 4 verses 17 and 19.

[35] Here is how I analyzed these three situations.

In situation (1) in our human flesh it is always easier to go along with the temptation then to resist it. Even in trying to resist temptation one thinks how he can comfort himself in the flesh to relieve the pressure. All this is temporary comfort. When we are tempted we need the Lord more than we think. Paul's temptations became stronger as he grew in faith. We all want the faith of Paul, but are we willing to receive beatings with whips and rods and being stoned and left for dead without complaining.

Here are some examples I have seen with others and my own life: At a Bible study in a restaurant a man bought all our meals but the next week we were given a check telling us it was not paid for. But everyone of us were witnesses that the man did pay. The waitress insisted the bill was not paid. The others were willing to pay but the man didn't want our help and ended up paying again but stopped coming to our group. A few weeks later the waitress was found cheating others and was fired. The man still had a spirit of vengeance. In my own personal experience I took out some health insurance where the agent made me a promise but didn't fulfill it. He did try for the next six months but he did nothing. I finally got so upset that I found another Insurance Company. I told the agent the story and he told me that he was a Christian and would never do anything like that. I signed up with that Company but soon after I found out he ignored my request. Now I am upset with two agents. I didn't learn my lesson the first time. Whenever a person had a wrong attitude he failed the temptation. Jesus was tempted three times with deceitfulness. Instead of overcoming the temptation with his power to correct the deceiver he chose to have the angels minister to Him. Remember Jesus was tempted no differently than we are.

[36] In situation (2) Jesus said the light will open the doors of salvation to the Gentiles. See Matthew 4:15-16 (above). It was true but it wouldn't happen until the Jews totally rejected their Messiah which was having Christ die on the cross. That is why Jesus didn't go outside his own nation. He was called only to the lost sheep of Israel. Matthew 10:5-6 "These twelve Jesus sent forth, and commanded them saying, go not into the way of the Gentiles and to any of the Samaritans enter not. But He answered and said, I am not sent but unto the lost sheep of Israel."

Jesus commanded his Disciples not to go to the Gentiles nor would He. This is why Jesus had an argument with the Jewish Leaders but He also told the people to do what the leaders told them but don't do what they do, for they were hypocrites. When Spiritual leaders use their power to kill Jesus they were using their civil power to come over the power of God's authority thinking they were doing God a service. This was the last straw. This is happening today. Just recently in my home town there was a court case where a church called, 'Word of Life' were trying to beat some sense into a rebellious person, the person ended up dying. The leaders will be serving time in prison. Many leaders think that there doctrinal authority overrides their own obedience to God. God is looking for obedience to His Word, not man made authority. Isn't it strange that among the fundamental churches today, new doctrine is continually coming into focus? So the big focus today is right doctrine and application is left out. Something that holds true all through the Old and the New Testament was obedience. The word doctrine is only found 12 times in the New Testament and Jesus said three times to beware of the doctrine of men. For the first 300 years after Christ, the Christian evangelized the four corners of the Roman Empire and about seven percent of the empire were saved. For the last few years Paul's ministry was restricted to only to the ones that came to him. I am not de-rating Paul's abilities but they were restricted in prison. The strange thing about it was the thousands of Christians that evangelized the Roman Empire, there was no central church giving them doctrine. But the churches were autonomous. This means, self-supporting self-governing and self-propagating. For the first 300 years after Christ this was how the church operated. They had different doctrines but had love that was willing to die. Today we want vengeance not God's love when there are disagreements.

[37] In situation (3) Everything lies on repentance and following Jesus. It is human nature to react

when others do us wrong. We are so mindful of their sin we can't see what is building up within ourselves. First there is anger, then bitterness and then vengeance. If we are not following Jesus we are in the path of no return. Until we go back to repentance we will even forget about our salvation. This is why we must live on forgiveness.

[38] **Matthew 6:14-15** *"*For if you forgive men their trespasses, your heavenly Father will also forgive you: [15] But if you forgive not men their trespasses, neither will your Father forgive you of your trespasses."

It is getting so that modern doctrine leaves this point out. They say God hates the wicked. And they have Scripture to back that up. **Psalm 5:5** "The foolish shall not stand: thou hates all workers of iniquity." We should never build doctrine on the Old Testament. In fact we should be careful not to form doctrine on the New Testament unless it is the way of Christ. Jesus is the way the truth and the life. **Matthew 5** has a large section on the changes from the Old and the New Testament. See **Matthew 5:43-44** p49 It clarifies the differences.

[39] In **Mathew 12:1-2**; What was Jesus accused of? How serious of a violation was it? Breaking the Sabbath was punishable by death.

[40] In **Matthew 12: 7** it says, if your know what this means, I desire mercy and not sacrifice, you would not condemn the innocent. It is like having speed laws. It is not to restrict us but they are for our own safety. Someone said, "morality can't be legislated

but behavior can be regulated." The law can't change the heart but they can restrain the heartless. So the internal is better than the external. A heart relationship with Jesus is priority over the law. Jesus saves not by the law. (see index Pg 56 for above Scriptures in [39] and [40] also [41] thru [45].

[41] What were these religious leaders emphasizing? The external at the expense of a relationship with God. Jesus gave reasons from the Old Testament. So the Pharisees would see grace over the law. In failing to see this simple truth they condemned Jesus to death because he made himself equal with God. **John 5:18**

[42] The High Priest asked Jesus, **Mark 26:63**, whether He was the Christ the son of God. And what did Jesus say? "You shall see the son of Man sitting on the right hand with power."

[43] And what did the High Priest do and say? **Matt. 2:65** He rent his clothes and said he blasphemed.

[44] And the High Priest asked the people. **Matthew 4:66** "What do you think? They answered, he is guilty of death.

[45] Jesus used the term, **Mark 2:27-28** "The Son of Man" for Himself, it is an Messianic term but why did he use this term? It is to explain the Sabbath was made for man and not man for the Sabbath, man is not made for a car but a car is made for Man. The Sabbath was to bless mankind. *In Romans, Paul changes the Old Testament Sabbath law in areas that were very strong in the Old Testament.*

Romans 14:1-4 *p17 Don't judge a man for what he thinks is right for God has given man that right.*

[46] The New Testament Sabbath has Freedom in Jesus, if you do not judge one another. The Old Testament had no toleration at all. When Jesus became the Lord of the Sabbath, it would be to benefit man. Yet men is never satisfied. For the first three hundred years after Christ the church was completely autonomous, by having their own doctrine, and yet others were trying to take away their freedom of what doctrine was right. Today the Catholic and evangelical doctrines are so different that most think we can't have the other attend our church because they are heathens. America was started by eleven different Evangelical doctrines that were so extremely different that each wanted preeminence in the Government. Roger Williams was the first to have tolerance for other religions. The puritans who came to the New World had no religious tolerance. In one survey, at the time of Christ over 70 Million Christians were killed because the church had no tolerance. And now each denominational group thought their doctrine was better. It is hard to be humble when one thinks his doctrine is the best.

[47] PAUL WAS CHOSEN TO GIVE THE LIGHT TO THE GENTILES AND ALSO REGULATED THE HOLY DAYS TO CONTINUE THE SABBATH INTO A NEW STRUCTURE CALLTHE HOLY DAY(S).

[48] The Jewish leaders were looking for a way to kill Jesus. They had two areas where Jesus was

breaking the Sabbath day rules. That was punishable by death and that is what they had in mind. They wanted Jesus dead because He had more followers than the Jewish leaders. They ended up killing him because Jesus said that He was the Son of God which made himself equal with God.

APPENDIX #1 - Large portions of Scripture in order by letters [A] to [F] p17-47
[A] New Testament Script. on the Sabbath p17-24
[B] Old Testament Script. on the Sabbath p24-36
[C] The Sermon on the Mount p37-40
[D] Matthew 4:1-20 p40-42
[E] Romans 14 p44-47
[F] Acts 10

[A] New Testament Scripture on the Sabbath.
Matthew 12:1-13 At that time Jesus went on the **Sabbath** day through the corn field; and his disciples were hungered, and began to pluck the ears of corn, and to eat. [2] But when the Pharisees saw *it*, they said unto him, Behold, thy disciples do that which is not lawful to do upon the **Sabbath** day. [3] But he said unto them, Have you not read what David did, when he was an hungered, and they that were with him; [4] How he entered into the house of God, and did eat the showbread, which was not lawful for him to eat, neither for them which were with him, but only for the priests? [5] Or have ye not

read in the law, how that on the **Sabbath** days the priests in the temple profane the **sabbath**, and are blameless? [6] But I say unto you, That in this place is *one* greater than the temple. [7] But if ye had known what *this* meaneth, I will have mercy, and not sacrifice, ye would not have condemned the guiltless. [8] For the Son of man is Lord even of the **Sabbath** day. [9] And when he was departed thence, he went into their synagogue: [10] And, behold, there was a man which had *his* hand withered. And they asked him, saying, Is it lawful to heal on the **Sabbath** days? that they might accuse him. [11] And he said unto them, What man shall there be among you, that shall have one sheep, and if it fall into a pit on the **Sabbath** day, will he not lay hold on it, and lift *it* out? [12] How much then is a man better than a sheep? Wherefore it is lawful to do well on the **Sabbath** days. [13] Then saith he to the man, Stretch forth thine hand. And he stretched *it* forth; and it was restored whole, like as the other.

Matthew 24:20 [20]But pray ye that your flight be not in the winter, neither on the **Sabbath** day:

Matthew 28:1 [1]In the end of the **Sabbath**, as it began to dawn toward the first *day* of the week, came Mary Magdalene and the other Mary to see the sepulchre.

Mark 1:2 As it is written in the prophets, Behold, I send my messenger before thy face, which shall prepare thy way before thee.

Mark 2:23-28
[23]And it came to pass, that he went through the corn

fields on the **Sabbath** day; and his disciples began, as they went, to pluck the ears of corn. [24] And the Pharisees said unto him, Behold, why do they on the **Sabbath** day that which is not lawful? [25]And he said unto them, Have ye never read what David did, when he had need, and was an hungered, he, and they that were with him? [26] How he went into the house of God in the days of Abiathar the high priest, and did eat the showbread, which is not lawful to eat but for the priests, and gave also to them which were with him? [27]And he said unto them, <u>The **Sabbath** was made for man, and not man for the **Sabbath**</u>: [28] Therefore <u>the Son of man is Lord also of the **Sabbath**.</u>

Mark 3:2-4 And they watched him, whether he would heal him on the **Sabbath** day; that they might accuse him. [3]And he saith unto the man which had the withered hand, Stand forth. [4]And he saith unto them, Is it lawful to do good on the **Sabbath** days, or to do evil? to save life, or to kill? But they held their peace.

Mark 15:42 And now when the even was come, because it was the preparation, that is, the day before the **Sabbath**,

Mark 16:1 And when the **Sabbath** was past, Mary Magdalene, and Mary the *mother* of James, and Salome, had bought sweet spices, that they might come and anoint him.

Luke 4:16 And he came to Nazareth, where he had been brought up: and, as his custom was, he went into the synagogue on the **Sabbath** day, and stood up for to read.

Luke 4:31 And came down to Capernaum, a city of Galilee, and taught them on the **Sabbath** days.

Luke 6:1 through Luke 6:9 ¹And it came to pass on the second **Sabbath** after the first, that he went through the corn fields; and his disciples plucked the ears of corn, and did eat, rubbing *them* in *their* hands. ²And certain of the Pharisees said unto them, Why do ye that which is not lawful to do on the Sabbath days? ³And Jesus answering them said, Have ye not read so much as this, what David did, when himself was an hungered, and they which were with him; ⁴How he went into the house of God, and did take and eat the showbread, and gave also to them that were with him; which it is not lawful to eat but for the priests alone? ⁵And he said unto them, That <u>the Son of man is Lord also of the</u> **<u>Sabbath</u>.** ⁶ And it came to pass also on another **Sabbath,** that he entered into the synagogue and taught: and there was a man whose right hand was withered. ⁷And the scribes and Pharisees watched him, whether he would heal on the **Sabbath** day; that they might find an accusation against him. ⁸But he knew their thoughts, and said to the man which had the withered hand, Rise up, and stand forth in the midst. And he arose and stood forth. ⁹ Then said Jesus unto them, I will ask you one thing; Is it lawful on the **Sabbath** days to do good, or to do evil? to save life, or to destroy *it*?

Luke 13:10-16 And he was teaching in one of the synagogues on the **Sabbath**. ¹¹And, behold, there was a woman which had a spirit of infirmity eighteen years, and was bowed together, and could in no wise lift up *herself*. ¹² And when Jesus saw her, he called *her to him*, and said unto her, Woman, thou art loosed from thine infirmity. ¹³And he laid *his* hands on her: and immediately she was made straight, and glorified God. ¹⁴And the ruler of the synagogue answered with indignation, because that Jesus had healed on the **Sabbath** day, and said unto the people, There are six days in which men ought to work: in them therefore come and be healed, and not on the **Sabbath** day. ¹⁵The Lord then answered him, and said, *Thou* hypocrite, doth not each one of you on the **Sabbath** loose his ox or *his* ass from the stall, and lead *him* away to watering? ¹⁶And ought not this woman, being a daughter of Abraham, whom Satan hath bound, lo, these eighteen years, be loosed from this bond on the day?

Luke 14:1-5 And it came to pass, as he went into the house of one of the chief Pharisees to eat bread on the **Sabbath** day, that they watched him. ²And, behold, there was a certain man before him which had the dropsy. ³And Jesus answering spake unto the lawyers and Pharisees, saying, Is it lawful to heal on the Sabbath day? ⁴And they held their peace. And he took *him*, and healed him, and let him go; ⁵And answered them, saying, Which of you shall have an ass or an ox fallen into a pit, and will not straightway pull him out on the **Sabbath** day?

Luke 23:54-56 And that day was the preparation, and the **Sabbath** drew on. [55]And the women also, which came with him from Galilee, followed after, and beheld the sepulchre, and how his body was laid. [56]And they returned, and prepared spices and ointments; and rested the **Sabbath day** according to the commandment.

John 5:9-18 And immediately the man was made whole, and took up his bed, and walked: and on the same day was the **Sabbath**. [10]The Jews therefore said unto him that was cured, It is the **Sabbath** day: it is not lawful for thee to carry *thy* bed. [11]He answered them, He that made me whole, the same said unto me, Take up thy bed, and walk. [12]Then asked they him, What man is that which said unto thee, Take up thy bed, and walk? [13]And he that was healed wist not who it was: for Jesus had conveyed himself away, a multitude being in *that* place. [14]Afterward Jesus findeth him in the temple, and said unto him, Behold, thou art made whole: sin no more, lest a worse thing come unto thee. [15]The man departed, and told the Jews that it was Jesus, which had made him whole. [16]And therefore did the Jews persecute Jesus, and sought to slay him, because he had done these things on the **sabbath** day. [17]But Jesus answered them, My Father worketh hitherto, and I work. [18]Therefore the Jews sought the more to kill him, because he not only had broken the

sabbath, but said also that God was his Father, making himself equal with God.

John 7:22-23 Moses therefore gave unto you circumcision; (not because it is of Moses, but of the fathers;) and ye on the **sabbath** day circumcise a man. ²³If a man on the **sabbath** day receive circumcision, that the law of Moses should not be broken; are ye angry at me, because I have made a man every whit whole on the **sabbath** day?

John 9:14-16 And it was the **sabbath** day when Jesus made the clay, and opened his eyes. ¹⁵Then again the Pharisees also asked him how he had received his sight. He said unto them, He put clay upon mine eyes, and I washed, and do see. ¹⁶Therefore said some of the Pharisees, This man is not of God, because he keepeth not the sabbath day. Others said, How can a man that is a sinner do such miracles? And there was a division among them.

John 19:31 The Jews therefore, because it was the preparation, that the bodies should not remain upon the cross on the **sabbath** day, (for that **sabbath** day was an high day,) besought Pilate that their legs might be broken, and *that* they might be taken away.***Philippians 2:5 to 8*** Let this mind be in you, which was also in Christ Jesus: ⁶ Who, being in the form of God, thought it not robbery to be equal with God: ⁷ But made himself of no reputation, and took upon him the form of a servant, and was made in the likeness of men: ⁸And being found in fashion as a man, he humbled himself, and became obedient unto death, even the death of the cross. For years I didn't do any personal work on Sunday's to keep the **Sabbath** day and I tried to restrict all personal pleasures.

[B] Old Testament Scripture on the Sabbath

Exodus 16:23-29 And he said unto them, This *is that* which the LORD hath said, To morrow *is* the rest of the holy **Sabbath** unto the LORD:

bake *that* which ye will bake *to day*, and seethe that ye will seethe; and that which remains over lay up for you to be kept until the morning. [24]And they laid it up till the morning, as Moses bade: and it did not stink, neither was there any worm therein. [25]And Moses said, eat that today; for to day *is* a **Sabbath** unto the LORD: to day ye shall not find it in the field. [26]Six days ye shall gather it; but on the seventh day, *which is* the **Sabbath,** in it there shall be none. [27]And it came to pass, *that* there went out *some* of the people on the seventh day for to gather, and they found none. [28]And the LORD said unto Moses, How long refuse ye to keep my commandments and my laws? [29]See, for that the LORD hath given you the **Sabbath**, therefore he giveth you on the sixth day the bread of two days; abide ye every man in his place, let no man go out of his place on the seventh day.

Exodus 20:8 through Exodus 20:11 Remember the **Sabbath** day, to keep it holy. [9]Six days shalt thou labor, and do all thy work: [10]But the seventh day *is* the **Sabbath** of the LORD thy God: *in it* thou shalt not do any work, thou, nor thy son, nor thy daughter, thy manservant, nor thy maidservant, nor thy cattle, nor thy stranger that *is* within thy gates: ¹¹For *in* six days the LORD made heaven and earth, the sea, and all that in them *is*, and rested the seventh day: wherefore the LORD blessed the **Sabbath** day, and hallowed it.

Exodus 31:13 Speak thou also unto the children of Israel, saying, Verily my **Sabbaths** ye shall keep: for it *is* a sign between me and you throughout your generations; that *ye* may know that I *am* the LORD that doth sanctify you.

Exodus 31:14 through Exodus 31:16
¹⁴Ye shall keep the **Sabbath** therefore; for it *is* holy unto you: every one that defileth it shall surely be put to death: for whosoever doeth *any* work therein, that soul shall be cut off from among his people. ¹⁵Six days may work be done; but in the seventh *is* the **Sabbath** of rest, holy to the LORD: whosoever doeth *any* work in the **Sabbath** day, he shall surely be put to death. ¹⁶Wherefore the children of Israel shall keep the **Sabbath**, to observe the **Sabbath** throughout their generations, *for* a perpetual covenant.

Exodus 35:2 through Exodus 35:3
²Six days shall work be done, but on the seventh day there shall be to you an holy day, a ***Sabbath*** of rest to the LORD: whosoever doeth work therein shall be put to death. ³Ye shall kindle no fire throughout your habitations upon the **Sabbath** day.

Leviticus 16:31
³¹It *shall be* a **Sabbath** of rest unto you, and ye shall afflict your souls, by a statute for ever.
Leviticus 19:3 Ye shall fear every man his mother, and his father, and keep my **Sabbath**s: I *am* the LORD your God.

Leviticus 19:30 Ye shall keep my **Sabbaths**, and reverence my sanctuary: I *am* the LORD.

Leviticus 23:3 Six days shall work be done: but the seventh day *is* the **Sabbath** of rest, an holy convocation; ye shall do no work *therein*: it *is* the **Sabbath** of the LORD in all your dwellings.
Leviticus 23:11 And he shall wave the sheaf before the LORD, to be accepted for you: on the morrow after the **Sabbath** the priest shall wave it.
Leviticus 23:15 through Leviticus 23:16
¹⁵And ye shall count unto you from the morrow after the **Sabbath**, from the day that ye brought the sheaf of the wave offering; seven **Sabbath**s shall be complete: ¹⁶Even unto the morrow after the seventh **Sabbath** shall ye number fifty days; and ye shall offer a new meat offering unto the LORD.
Leviticus 23:24 Speak unto the children of Israel, saying, In the seventh month, in the first *day* of the month, shall ye have a **Sabbath**, a memorial of blowing of trumpets, an holy convocation.
Leviticus 23:32 It *shall be* unto you a **Sabbath** of rest, and ye shall afflict your souls: in the ninth *day* of the month at even, from even unto even, shall ye celebrate your **Sabbath**.

Leviticus 23:39 Also in the fifteenth day of the seventh month, when ye have gathered in the fruit of the land, ye shall keep a feast unto the LORD seven days: on the first day *shall be* a **Sabbath,** and on the eighth day *shall be* a **Sabbath**.

Leviticus 24:8 Every **Sabbath** he shall set it in order before the LORD continually, *being taken* from the children of Israel by an everlasting covenant.

Leviticus 25:1-8 And the LORD spake unto Moses in mount Sinai, saying, ²Speak unto the children of Israel, and say unto them, When ye come into the land which I give you, then shall the land keep a **Sabbath** unto the LORD. ³Six years thou shalt sow thy field, and six years thou shalt prune thy vineyard, and gather in the fruit thereof; ⁴But in the seventh year shall be a **Sabbath** of rest unto the land, a **Sabbath** for the LORD: thou shalt neither sow thy field, nor prune thy vineyard. ⁵That which groweth of its own accord of thy harvest thou shalt not reap, neither gather the grapes of thy vine undressed: *for* it is a year of rest unto the land. ⁶And the Sabbath of the land shall be meat for you; for thee, and for thy servant, and for thy maid, and for thy hired servant, and for thy stranger that sojourneth with thee, ⁷And for thy cattle, and for the beast that *are* in thy land, shall all the increase thereof be meat.

⁸And thou shalt number seven **Sabbaths** of years unto thee, seven times seven years; and the space of the seven **Sabbaths** of years shall be unto thee forty and nine years.

Leviticus 26:2 Ye shall keep my **Sabbath**s, and reverence my sanctuary: I *am* the LORD.

Numbers 15:32 And while the children of Israel were in the wilderness, they found a man that gathered sticks upon the **Sabbath** day.

Numbers 28:9-10 And on the **Sabbath** day two lambs of the first year without spot, and two tenth deals of flour *for* a meat offering, mingled with oil, and the drink offering thereof: [10]*This is* the burnt offering of every **Sabbath**, beside the continual burnt offering, and his drink offering.

Deuteronomy 5:13-15 Six days thou shalt labour, and do all thy work: [14]But the seventh day *is* the **Sabbath** of the LORD thy God: *in it* thou shalt not do any work, thou, nor thy son, nor thy daughter, nor thy manservant, nor thy maidservant, nor thine ox, nor thine ass, nor any of thy cattle, nor thy stranger that *is* within thy gates; that thy manservant and thy maidservant may rest as well as thou. [15]And remember that thou wast a servant in the land of Egypt, and *that* the LORD thy God brought thee out thence through a mighty hand and by a stretched out arm: therefore the LORD thy God commanded thee to keep the **Sabbath** day.

1 Chronicles 9:32 And *other* of their brethren, of the sons of the Kohathites, *were* over the showbread, to prepare *it* every **Sabbath**.

1 Chronicles 23:31 And to offer all burnt sacrifices unto the LORD in the **Sabbath**s, in the new moons, and on the set feasts, by number, according to the order commanded unto them, continually before the LORD:

2 Chronicles 2:4 Behold, I build an house to the name of the LORD my God, to dedicate *it* to him, *and* to burn before him sweet incense, and for the continual showbread, and for the burnt offerings morning and evening, on the **Sabbaths**, and on the new moons, and on the solemn feasts of the LORD our God. This *is an ordinance* for ever to Israel.

2 Chronicles 8:13 Even after a certain rate every day, offering according to the commandment of Moses, on the **Sabbaths**, and on the new moons, and on the solemn feasts, three times in the year, *even* in the feast of unleavened bread, and in the feast of weeks, and in the feast of tabernacles.

2 Chronicles 23:4-8 This *is* the thing that ye shall do; A third part of you entering on the **Sabbath,** of the priests and of the Levites, *shall be* porters of the doors; [5]And a third part *shall be* at the king's house; and a third part at the gate of the foundation: and all the people *shall be* in the courts of the house of the LORD. [6]But let none come into the house of the LORD, save the priests, and they that minister of the Levites; they shall go in, for they *are* holy: but all the people shall keep the watch of the LORD. [7]And the Levites shall compass the king round about, every man with his weapons in his hand; and whosoever *else* cometh into the house, he shall be put to death: but be ye with the king when he cometh in, and when he goeth out. [8]So the Levites and all Judah did according to all things that

Jehoiada the priest had commanded, and took every man his men that were to come in on the **Sabbath,** with them that were to go *out* on the **Sabbath:** for Jehoiada the priest dismissed not the courses.

2 Chronicles 31:3 He appointed also the king's portion of his substance for the burnt offerings, *to wit*, for the morning and evening burnt offerings, and the burnt offerings for the **Sabbaths**, and for the new moons, and for the set feasts, as *it is* written in the law of the LORD.

2 Chronicles 36:21
 To fulfil the word of the LORD by the mouth of Jeremiah, until the land had enjoyed her **Sabbath**s: *for* as long as she lay desolate she kept **Sabbath**, to fulfil threescore and ten years.

Nehemiah 9:14 And madest known unto them thy holy **Sabbath,** and commandedst them precepts, statutes, and laws, by the hand of Moses thy servant:

Nehemiah 10:31 And *if* the people of the land bring ware or any victuals on the **Sabbath** day to sell, *that* we would not buy it of them on the **Sabbath,** or on the holy day: and *that* we would leave the seventh year, and the exaction of every debt.

Nehemiah 10:33 For the showbread, and for the continual meat offering, and for the continual burnt offering, of the **Sabbaths**, of the new moons, for the set feasts, and for the holy *things*, and for the sin offerings to make an atonement for Israel, and *for* all the work of the house of our God.

Nehemiah 13:15 through Nehemiah 13:19
¹⁵In those days saw I in Judah *some* treading wine presses on the **Sabbath,** and bringing in sheaves, and lading asses; as also wine, grapes, and figs, and all *manner of* burdens, which they brought into Jerusalem on the **Sabbath** day: and I testified *against them* in the day wherein they sold victuals. ¹⁶There dwelt men of Tyre also therein, which brought fish, and all manner of ware, and sold on the **Sabbath** unto the children of Judah, and in Jerusalem. ¹⁷Then I contended with the nobles of Judah, and said unto them, What evil thing *is* this that ye do, and profane the **Sabbath** day? ¹⁸Did not your fathers thus, and did not our God bring all this evil upon us, and upon this city? yet ye bring more wrath upon Israel by profaning the **Sabbath.** ¹⁹And it came to pass, that when the gates of Jerusalem began to be dark before the **Sabbath,** I commanded that the gates should be shut, and charged that they should not be opened till after the **Sabbath**: and *some* of my servants set I at the gates, *that* there should no burden be brought in on the Sabbath day.

Nehemiah 13:21 Then I testified against them, and said unto them, Why lodge ye about the wall? if ye do *so* again, I will lay hands on you. From that time forth came they no *more* on the **Sabbath**.

Nehemiah 13:22 And I commanded the Levites that they should cleanse themselves, and *that* they should come *and* keep the gates, to sanctify the **Sabbath** day. Remember me, O my God,

concerning this also, and spare me according to the greatness of thy mercy.
Isaiah 1:13 Bring no more vain oblations; incense is an abomination unto me; the new moons and **Sabbaths**, the calling of assemblies, I cannot away with; *it is* iniquity, even the solemn meeting.
Isaiah 56:2-:6 Blessed *is* the man *that* doeth this, and the son of man *that* layeth hold on it; that keepeth the **Sabbath** from polluting it, and keepeth his hand from doing any evil.³Neither let the son of the stranger, that hath joined himself to the LORD, speak, saying, The LORD hath utterly separated me from his people: neither let the eunuch say, Behold, I *am* a dry tree. ⁴For thus saith the LORD unto the eunuchs that keep my **Sabbaths**, and choose *the things* that please me, and take hold of my covenant; ⁵Even unto them will I give in mine house and within my walls a place and a name better than of sons and of daughters: I will give them an everlasting name, that shall not be cut off. ⁶Also the sons of the stranger, that join themselves to the LORD, to serve him, and to love the name of the LORD, to be his servants, every one that keepeth the **Sabbath** from polluting it, and taketh hold of my covenant;
*Isaiah 58:13*If thou turn away thy foot from the **Sabbath**, *from* doing thy pleasure on my holy day; and call the **Sabbath** a delight, the holy of the LORD, honourable; and shalt honour him, not doing thine own ways, nor finding thine own pleasure, nor speaking *thine own* words:

Isaiah 66:23 And it shall come to pass, *that* from one new moon to another, and from one **Sabbath** to another, shall all flesh come to worship before me, saith the LORD.

Jeremiah 17:21 through Jeremiah 17:27 Thus saith the LORD; Take heed to yourselves, and bear no burden on the **Sabbath** day, nor bring *it* in by the gates of Jerusalem; ²²Neither carry forth a burden out of your houses on the **Sabbath** day, neither do ye any work, but hallow ye the ***Sabbath*** day, as I commanded your fathers. ²³But they obeyed not, neither inclined their ear, but made their neck stiff, that they might not hear, nor receive instruction. ²⁴And it shall come to pass, if ye diligently hearken unto me, saith the LORD, to bring in no burden through the gates of this city on the **Sabbath** day, but hallow the **Sabbath** day, to do no work therein; ²⁵Then shall there enter into the gates of this city kings and princes sitting upon the throne of David, riding in chariots and on horses, they, and their princes, the men of Judah, and the inhabitants of Jerusalem: and this city shall remain for ever. ²⁶And they shall come from the cities of Judah, and from the places about Jerusalem, and from the land of Benjamin, and from the plain, and from the mountains, and from the south, bringing burnt offerings, and sacrifices, and meat offerings, and incense, and bringing sacrifices of praise, unto the house of the LORD. ²⁷But if ye will not hearken unto me to hallow the **Sabbath** day, and not to bear a burden, even entering in at the gates of Jerusalem on the **Sabbath** day; then will I kindle a fire in the gates thereof, and it shall devour the palaces of Jerusalem, and it shall not be quenched.

Lamentations 1:7 Jerusalem remembered in the days of her affliction and of her miseries all her pleasant things that she had in the days of old, when her people fell into the hand of the enemy, and none did help her: the adversaries saw her, *and* did mock at her **Sabbath**s.

Lamentations 2:6 And he hath violently taken away his tabernacle, as *if it were of* a garden: he hath destroyed his places of the assembly: the LORD hath caused the solemn feasts and **Sabbaths** to be forgotten in Zion, and hath despised in the indignation of his anger the king and the priest.

Ezekiel 20:12-13 Moreover also I gave them my **Sabbaths**, to be a sign between me and them, that they might know that I *am* the LORD that sanctify them. [13]But the house of Israel rebelled against me in the wilderness: they walked not in my statutes, and they despised my judgments, which *if* a man do, he shall even live in them; and my **Sabbaths** they greatly polluted: then I said, I would pour out my fury upon them in the wilderness, to consume them.

Ezekiel 20:11 And I gave them my statutes, and showed them my judgments, which *if* a man do, he shall even live in them. [12]Moreover also I gave them my **Sabbath**s, to be a sign between me and them, that they might know that I *am* the LORD that sanctify them. [13]But the house of Israel rebelled against me in the wilderness: they walked not in my statutes, and they despised my judgments, which *if* a man do, he shall even live in them; and my **Sabbaths** they greatly polluted: then I said, I would pour out my fury upon them in the wilderness, to consume them.

Ezekiel 20:16 Because they despised my judgments, and walked not in my statutes, but polluted my **Sabbaths**: for their heart went after their idols.

Ezekiel 20:20 And hallow my **Sabbaths**; and they shall be a sign between me and you, that ye may know that I *am* the LORD your God.

Ezekiel 20:21 Notwithstanding the children rebelled against me: they walked not in my statutes, neither kept my judgments to do them, which *if* a man do, he shall even live in them; they polluted my **Sabbaths**: then I said, I would pour out my fury upon them, to accomplish my anger against them in the wilderness.

Ezekiel 20:24 Because they had not executed my judgments, but had despised my statutes, and had polluted my **Sabbaths**, and their eyes were after their fathers' idols..

Ezekiel 44:24 And in controversy they shall stand in judgment; *and* they shall judge it according to my judgments: and they shall keep my laws and my statutes in all mine assemblies; and they shall hallow my **Sabbath**s.

Ezekiel 45:17 And it shall be the prince's part *to give* burnt offerings, and meat offerings, and drink offerings, in the feasts, and in the new moons, and in the **Sabbath**s, in all solemnities of the house of Israel: he shall prepare the sin offering, and the meat offering, and the burnt offering, and the peace offerings, to make reconciliation for the house of Israel.

Ezekiel 46:1- 4 Thus saith the Lord GOD; The gate of the inner court that looketh toward the east shall be shut the six working days; but on the **Sabbath** it shall be opened, and in the day of the new moon it shall be opened.. ³Likewise the people of the land shall worship at the door of this gate before the LORD in the **Sabbath**s and in the new moons. ⁴And the burnt offering that the prince shall offer unto the LORD in the **Sabbath** day *shall be* six lambs without blemish, and a ram without blemish.

Ezekiel 46:12 Now when the prince shall prepare a voluntary burnt offering or peace offerings voluntarily unto the LORD, *one* shall then open him the gate that looketh toward the east, and he shall prepare his burnt offering and his peace offerings, as he did on the **Sabbath** day: then he shall go forth; and after his going forth *one* shall shut the gate.

Amos 8:5 Saying, When will the new moon be gone, that we may sell corn? and the **Sabbath,** that we may set forth wheat, making the ephah small, and the shekel great, and falsifying the balances by deceit?

[C] The Sermon on the Mount - Chapter 5

¹And seeing the multitudes, he went up into a mountain: and when he was set, his disciples came unto him: ²And he opened his mouth, and taught them, saying, ³Blessed *are* the poor in spirit: for theirs is the kingdom of heaven. ⁴Blessed *are* they that mourn: for they shall be comforted. ⁵Blessed *are* the meek: for they shall inherit the earth. ⁶Blessed *are* they which do hunger and thirst after righteousness: for they shall be filled. ⁷Blessed *are* the merciful: for they shall obtain mercy. ⁸Blessed *are* the pure in heart: for they shall see God. ⁹Blessed *are* the peacemakers: for they shall be called the children of God. ¹⁰Blessed *are* they which are persecuted for righteousness' sake: for theirs is the kingdom of heaven. ¹¹ Blessed are you, when *men* shall revile you, and persecute *you*, and shall say all manner of evil against you falsely, for my sake. ¹² Rejoice, and be exceeding glad: for great *is* your reward in heaven: for so persecuted they the prophets which were before you.

¹⁷ Think not that I am come to destroy the law, or the prophets: I am not come to destroy, but to fulfil. ¹⁸ For surely I say unto you, Until heaven and earth pass, one jot or one tittle shall in no wise pass from the law, till all be fulfilled.

¹⁹ Whosoever therefore shall break one of these least commandments, and shall teach men so, he

shall be called the least in the kingdom of heaven: but whosoever shall do and teach *them*, the same shall be called great in the kingdom of heaven.

20 For I say unto you, except your righteousness shall exceed *the righteousness* of the scribes and Pharisees, you shall in no case enter into the kingdom of heaven.

21 You have heard that it was said by them of old time, Thou shalt not kill; and whosoever shall kill shall be in danger of the judgment: 22 But I say unto you, That whosoever is angry with his brother without a cause shall be in danger of the judgment: and whosoever shall say to his brother, Raca, shall be in danger of the council: but whosoever shall say, Thou fool, shall be in danger of hell fire. 23 Therefore if thou bring thy gift to the altar, and there remember that thy brother hath ought against thee; 24 Leave there thy gift before the altar, and go thy way; first be reconciled to thy brother, and then come and offer thy gift. 25 Agree with thine adversary quickly, while you art in the way with him; lest at any time the adversary deliver thee to the judge, and the judge deliver thee to the officer, and thou be cast into prison. 26 Surely I say unto thee, Thou shalt by no means come out, till thou hast paid the uttermost farthing.

27 Ye have heard that it was said by them of old time, Thou shalt not commit adultery: 28 But I say unto you, That whosoever looks on a woman to lust after her hath committed adultery with her already in his heart. 29 And if thy right eye offend thee, pluck it

out, and cast *it* from thee: for it is profitable for thee that one of thy members should perish, and not *that* thy whole body should be cast into hell. ³⁰ And if thy right hand offend thee, cut it off, and cast *it* from thee: for it is profitable for thee that one of thy members should perish, and not *that* thy whole body should be cast into hell. ³¹ It hath been said, Whosoever shall put away his wife, let him give her a writing of divorcement: ³² But I say unto you, That whosoever shall put away his wife, saving for the cause of fornication, causes her to commit adultery: and whosoever shall marry her that is divorced has committed adultery. ³³ Again, ye have heard that it hath been said by them of old time, Thou shalt not forswear thyself, but shalt perform unto the Lord thine oaths: ³⁴ But I say unto you, Swear not at all; neither by heaven; for it is God's throne: ³⁵ Nor by the earth; for it is his footstool: neither by Jerusalem; for it is the city of the great King. ³⁶ Neither shalt thou swear by thy head, because you can not make one hair white or black. ³⁷ But let your communication be, Yes; or no: for whatsoever is more than these comes of evil. ³⁸ You have heard that it hath been said, An eye for an eye, and a tooth for a tooth: ³⁹ But I say unto you, resist not evil: but whosoever shall hit you on thy right cheek, turn to him the other also. ⁴⁰ And if any man will sue thee at the law, and take away thy coat, let him have *thy* cloak also. ⁴¹ And whosoever compels you to go a mile, go with him two miles. ⁴² Give to him that asks you, and from him that would borrow from you turn not away.

<u>⁴³ Ye have heard that it has been said, you shalt love thy neighbor, and hate thine enemy. ⁴⁴ But I say unto you, Love your enemies, bless them that curse you, do good to them that hate you, and pray for them which despitefully use you, and persecute you;</u> ⁴⁵ That ye may be the children of your Father which is in heaven: for he makes His sun to rise on the evil and on the good, and sends rain on the just and on the unjust. ⁴⁶ For if ye love them which love you, what reward have you? Do not even the publicans do the same? ⁴⁷And if ye salute your brethren only, what do you more *than others*? do not even the publicans do the same? ⁴⁸ Be perfect, even as your Father which is in heaven is perfect.

Did Christ have any changes over the Sabbath Old Testament law. We know that the Ten Commandments is the only part of the Bible God wrote with his own finger. We must conclude what God writes with his own hand must be important for both the Old and New Testament, unless He said differently.

[D] Matthew 4:1-20 Then was Jesus led up of the Spirit into the wilderness to be tempted of the devil. ² And when he had fasted forty days and forty nights, he was afterward an hungered. ³ And when the tempter came to him, he said, If thou be the Son of God, command that these stones be made bread.

⁴ But he answered and said, It is written, Man shall not live by bread alone, but by every word that proceeded out of the mouth of God. ⁵ Then the devil taketh him up into the holy city, and setteth him on a pinnacle of the temple, ⁶ And said unto him, If thou be the Son of God, cast thyself down: for it is written, He shall give his angels charge concerning thee: and in *their* hands they shall bear thee up, lest at any time thou dash thy foot against a stone. ⁷ Jesus said unto him, It is written again, Thou shalt not tempt the Lord thy God. ⁸ Again, the devil taketh him up into an exceeding high mountain, and showed him all the kingdoms of the world, and the glory of them; ⁹ And said unto him, All these things will I give thee, if thou wilt fall down and worship me. ¹⁰ Then said Jesus unto him, Get thee hence, Satan: for it is written, Thou shalt worship the Lord thy God, and him only shalt thou serve. ¹¹ Then the devil leaves him, and, behold, angels came and ministered unto him. ¹² Now when Jesus had heard that John was cast into prison, he departed into Galilee; ¹³ And leaving Nazareth, he came and dwelt in Capernaum, which is upon the sea coast, in the borders of Zabulon and Nephthalim: ¹⁴ That it might be fulfilled which was spoken by Esaias the prophet, saying, ¹⁵ The land of Zabulon, and the land of Nephthalim, *by* the way of the sea, beyond Jordan, Galilee of the Gentiles; ¹⁶ The people which sat in darkness saw great light; and to them which sat in

the region and shadow of death light is sprung up. [17] From that time Jesus began to preach, and to say, Repent: for the kingdom of heaven is at hand. [18] And Jesus, walking by the sea of Galilee, saw two brethren, Simon called Peter, and Andrew his brother, casting a net into the sea: for they were fishers. [19] And he said unto them, Follow me, and I will make you fishers of men. [20] And they straightway left *their* nets, and followed him.

[E] Romans 14 (whole chapter)

Romans 14 [1] Him that is weak in the faith receive ye, *but* not to doubtful disputations. [2] For one believeth that he may eat all things: another, who is weak, eateth herbs. [3] Let not him that eateth despise him that eateth not; and let not him which eateth not judge him that eateth: for God hath received him. [4] Who art thou that judgest another man's servant? to his own master he standeth or falleth. Yea, he shall be holden up: for God is able to make him stand. [5] One man esteemeth one day above another: another esteemeth every day *alike*. Let every man be fully persuaded in his own mind. [6] He that regardeth the day, regardeth *it* unto the Lord; and he that regardeth not the day, to the Lord he doth not regard *it*. He that eateth, eateth to the Lord, for he giveth God thanks; and he that eateth not, to the Lord he eateth not, and giveth God thanks. [7] For none of us liveth to himself, and no man dieth to himself. [8] For whether we live, we live unto the Lord; and whether we die, we die unto the

Lord: whether we live therefore, or die, we are the Lord's. ⁹ For to this end Christ both died, and rose, and revived, that he might be Lord both of the dead and living. ¹⁰ But why dost thou judge thy brother? or why dost thou set at nought thy brother? for we shall all stand before the judgment seat of Christ. ¹¹ For it is written, *As* I live, saith the Lord, every knee shall bow to me, and every tongue shall confess to God. ¹² So then every one of us shall give account of himself to God. ¹³ Let us not therefore judge one another any more: but judge this rather, that no man put a stumblingblock or an occasion to fall in *his* brother's way. ¹⁴ I know, and am persuaded by the Lord Jesus, that *there is* nothing unclean of itself: but to him that esteemeth any thing to be unclean, to him *it is* unclean. ¹⁵ But if thy brother be grieved with *thy* meat, now walkest thou not charitably. Destroy not him with thy meat, for whom Christ died. ¹⁶ Let not then your good be evil spoken of: ¹⁷ For the kingdom of God is not meat and drink; but righteousness, and peace, and joy in the Holy Ghost. ¹⁸ For he that in these things serveth Christ *is* acceptable to God, and approved of men. ¹⁹ Let us therefore follow after the things which make for peace, and things wherewith one may edify another. ²⁰ For meat destroy not the work of God. All things indeed *are* pure; but *it is* evil for that man who eateth with offence. ²¹ *It is* good neither to eat flesh, nor to drink wine, nor *any thing* whereby thy brother stumbleth, or is offended, or is made weak. ²² Hast thou faith? have *it* to thyself before God. Happy *is* he that condemneth not himself in that thing which he alloweth. ²³ And he that doubteth is damned if he eat, because *he eateth* not of faith: for whatsoever *is* not of faith is sin.

Back in the 1940's the blue laws were made to respect the Sabbath. First Sunday was made the Sabbath in honor of Christ since it was the day of Resurrection. And to make it a day of rest, all store by law had to be closed and there was no professional sports allowed on Sunday.

[F] Acts 10:1-48

¹There was a certain man in Caesarea called Cornelius, a centurion of the band called the Italian *band*, ²A devout *man*, and one that feared God with all his house, which gave much alms to the people, and prayed to God alway. ³He saw in a vision evidently about the ninth hour of the day an angel of God coming in to him, and saying unto him, Cornelius. ⁴And when he looked on him, he was afraid, and said, What is it, Lord? And he said unto him, Thy prayers and thine alms are come up for a memorial before God. ⁵And now send men to Joppa, and call for *one* Simon, whose surname is Peter: ⁶He lodgeth with one Simon a tanner, whose house is by the sea side: he shall tell thee what thou oughtest to do. ⁷And when the angel which spake unto Cornelius was departed, he called two of his household servants, and a devout soldier of them that waited on him continually; ⁸And when he had declared all *these* things unto them, he sent them to Joppa.

⁹On the morrow, as they went on their journey, and drew nigh unto the city, Peter went up upon the housetop to pray

about the sixth hour: [10]And he became very hungry, and would have eaten: but while they made ready, he fell into a trance, [11]And saw heaven opened, and a certain vessel descending unto him, as it had been a great sheet knit at the four corners, and let down to the earth: [12]Wherein were all manner of fourfooted beasts of the earth, and wild beasts, and creeping things, and fowls of the air. [13]And there came a voice to him, Rise, Peter; kill, and eat. [14]But Peter said, Not so, Lord; for I have never eaten any thing that is common or unclean. [15]And the voice *spake* unto him again the second time, What God hath cleansed, *that* call not thou common. [16]This was done thrice: and the vessel was received up again into heaven. [17]Now while Peter doubted in himself what this vision which he had seen should mean, behold, the men which were sent from Cornelius had made inquiry for Simon's house, and stood before the gate, [18]And called, and asked whether Simon, which was surnamed Peter, were lodged there.

[19]While Peter thought on the vision, the Spirit said unto him, Behold, three men seek thee. [20]Arise therefore, and get thee down, and go with them, doubting nothing: for I have sent them. [21]Then Peter went down to the men which were sent unto him from Cornelius; and said, Behold, I am he whom ye seek: what *is* the cause wherefore ye are come? [22]And they said, Cornelius the centurion, a just man, and one that feareth God, and of good report among all the nation of the Jews, was warned from God by an holy angel to send for thee into his house, and to hear words of thee. [23]Then called he them in, and lodged *them*. And on the morrow Peter went away with them, and certain brethren from Joppa accompanied him. [24]And the morrow after they entered into Caesarea. And Cornelius waited for them, and had called together his kinsmen and near

friends. ²⁵And as Peter was coming in, Cornelius met him, and fell down at his feet, and worshipped *him*. ²⁶But Peter took him up, saying, Stand up; I myself also am a man. ²⁷And as he talked with him, he went in, and found many that were come together. ²⁸And he said unto them, Ye know how that it is an unlawful thing for a man that is a Jew to keep company, or come unto one of another nation; but God hath showed me that I should not call any man common or unclean. ²⁹Therefore came I *unto you* without gainsaying, as soon as I was sent for: I ask therefore for what intent ye have sent for me? ³⁰And Cornelius said, Four days ago I was fasting until this hour; and at the ninth hour I prayed in my house, and, behold, a man stood before me in bright clothing, ³¹And said, Cornelius, thy prayer is heard, and thine alms are had in remembrance in the sight of God. ³²Send therefore to Joppa, and call hither Simon, whose surname is Peter; he is lodged in the house of *one* Simon a tanner by the sea side: who, when he cometh, shall speak unto thee. ³³Immediately therefore I sent to thee; and thou hast well done that thou art come. Now therefore are we all here present before God, to hear all things that are commanded thee of God.

³⁴Then Peter opened *his* mouth, and said, Of a truth I perceive that God is no respecter of persons: ³⁵But in every nation he that feareth him, and worketh righteousness, is accepted with him. ³⁶The word which *God* sent unto the children of Israel, preaching peace by Jesus Christ: (he is Lord of all:) ³⁷That word, *I say*, ye know, which was published throughout all Judaea, and began from Galilee, after the baptism which John preached; ³⁸How God anointed Jesus of Nazareth with the Holy Ghost and with power: who went about doing good, and healing all that were oppressed of the devil; for

God was with him. ^{39}And we are witnesses of all things which he did both in the land of the Jews, and in Jerusalem; whom they slew and hanged on a tree: ^{40}Him God raised up the third day, and showed him openly; ^{41}Not to all the people, but unto witnesses chosen before of God, *even* to us, who did eat and drink with him after he rose from the dead. ^{42}And he commanded us to preach unto the people, and to testify that it is he which was ordained of God *to be* the Judge of quick and dead. ^{43}To him give all the prophets witness, that through his name whosoever believeth in him shall receive remission of sins.

^{44}While Peter yet spake these words, the Holy Ghost fell on all them which heard the word. ^{45}And they of the circumcision which believed were astonished, as many as came with Peter, because that on the Gentiles also was poured out the gift of the Holy Ghost. ^{46}For they heard them speak with tongues, and magnify God. Then answered Peter, ^{47}Can any man forbid water, that these should not be baptized, which have received the Holy Ghost as well as we? ^{48}And he commanded them to be baptized in the name of the Lord. Then prayed they him to tarry certain days.

Apendix #2 The paragraph number in brackets is on the left side of the Scriptures

[2] Matthew 10:5 ^{5} These twelve Jesus sent forth, and commanded them, saying, Go not into the way of the Gentiles, and into *any* city of the Samaritans enter ye not:

Matthew 15:22-24 And behold a woman of Cannaan came out of the same coasts and cried unto Him saying, have mercy on me, O Lord thou son of David my daughter Is grievously vexed with a devil. [23] But he answered her not a word. And his disciples came and besought him, saying, Send her away; for she cried after us. [24] But he answered and said, I am not sent but unto the lost sheep of the house of Israel

[6] Romans 6:5 "For if we have been united together in the likeness of His death we shall be also in the likeness of His resurrection."

[7] Acts 9:15 Acts 9:15 But the Lord said unto him Go the way, for he is a chosen vessel unto me, to bear my name before the Gentiles, and Kings and the children of Israel

[8] I Corinthians 13:3 An thought I bestow all my goods to feed the poor and thought I give my body to be burned and have not love it profits me nothing

[13] Scripture on loving them that do not love you. Below

[13] Matthew 5:10-13 Blessed are they which are persecuted for righteousness sake for theirs is the kingdom of heaven. 11 ?Blessed are ye, when men shall revile you and persecute you and shall say all manner of evil against you falsely for my sake. 13 Rejoice and be exceeding glad for great is your reward in heaven for so persecuted they the prophets which were before you.

[13] Matthew 5:21-22 [21]Ye have heard that it was said by them of old time, Thou shalt not kill; and whosoever shall kill shall be in danger of the judgment: ^{22}But I say unto you, That whosoever is angry with his brother without a cause shall be in danger of the judgment: and whosoever shall say to his brother, Raca, shall be in danger of the council: but whosoever shall say, Thou fool, shall be in danger of hell fire.

[13] **Matthew 5:27-28** ^{27}Ye have heard that it was said by them of old time, Thou shalt not commit adultery: ^{28}But I say unto you, That whosoever looketh on a woman to lust after her hath committed adultery with her already in his heart.

[13] **Matthew 5:39-41** ^{39}But I say unto you, That ye resist not evil: but whosoever shall smite thee on thy right cheek, turn to him the other also. ^{40}And if any man will sue thee at the law, and take away thy coat, let him have *thy* cloak also. ^{41}And whosoever shall compel thee to go a mile, go with him twain. ^{42}Give to him that asketh thee, and from him that would borrow of thee turn not thou away.

[13] **Matthew 5:43-44** ^{43}Ye have heard that it hath been said, Thou shalt love thy neighbour, and hate thine enemy. ^{44}But I say unto you, Love your enemies, bless them that curse you, do good to them that hate you, and pray for them which despitefully use you, and persecute you;

[15] **Romans 6:5** For if we have been planted together in the likeness of his death we shall be also in the likeness of his resurrection

[17] **Acts 9:15** But the Lord said unto him Go the way, for he is a chosen vessel unto me, to bear my

name before the Gentiles, and Kings and the children of Israel

[18] Acts 9:4 Then Paul fell to the ground and heard a voice saying to him. Saul. Saul why are you persecuting Me? This was far from the only time Paul had to suffer for the Lord Jesus.

[24] Galatians 5:22-23 is: The fruit of the spirit is: Love, joy peace, patience, gentleness, goodness, faith, meekness and temperance which means self-control.

[30] I Corinthians 11:31 "for if we would judge ourselves we should not be judged."

said, I am not sent but unto the lost sheep of the house of Israel

Summary

There are 613 laws in the Old Testament. Some of them are in the New Testament but have been changed by Jesus in the New Testament. These changes are found in the four Gospels: Matthew, Mark, Luke and John but also in the book of Romans by the Apostle Paul. Jesus gave Paul the authority to so, by the Holy Spirit. The Holy Spirit works in to continue the work of Jesus after He was crucified. Here are some of the changes that were made in the New Testament. The Ten Commandments are the only part of the Bible which was written by the finger of God. He had to do it twice because of the rebellion of the people and the anger of Moses. It probably was more because of the anger of Moses because he didn't seem to have love for the people when He broke the first tablets of the Ten Commandments.

[50] The Old Testament laws had little grace and mercy. Judgement was met with immediate death. The New Testament commandments of Christ had grace and forgiveness many times. Jesus told his disciples to forgive 7 times 70. I can't count the number of times of asking for forgiveness; neither can I count the times I didn't ask for forgiveness and I should have. The first thing Jesus said was: "repent for the kingdom of Heaven is at hand." So asking for forgiveness is very necessary. Not only for salvation but also in daily living. All the New Testament law under grace seems to be much easier but the hard part is know: not only wrong actions are sin but under grace having wrong thoughts are also sin. Jesus said whosoever in angry without cause, (meaning without love,) has already committed murder. Also who so ever looks upon a woman with lust has already committed adultery. All sin is based on lust and the pride of life. **I john 2:15-16** p61

[51] We shouldn't recognize any law as sin in the Old Testament if it was not backed up with the New Testament. The 10 Commandments were back up by what Jesus did and said.

Most of the law in the Old Testament has been eliminated or changed. An example of this is in **Matthew 5:43-44**. P61 Where Jesus explained that the Old Testament said to love your neighbor and hate your enemy, but under grace the command is to love our enemy.

Some of the laws in the Old Testament had judgement right on the spot and the guilty were stoned to death. In another example in the Old Testament there were 1,500 regulations in what the Sabbath Day restricted. Just to break one of these regulations was punished by stoning. Jesus said that He was Lord of the Sabbath. That didn't do away with the Sabbath day but the Sabbath Day is called a holy day. <u>See Roman 14 in the appendix</u>.

[52] The laws in the Old Testament were like the laws of a modern nation. Force was use when there was disobedience. In fact the church at that time had the power of the government and millions were put to death because of not adhering to the law. The State church started to diminish that when America became a country. That was over 1700 years after Christ came the first time. Why did God allow that to continue so long? The Lord wanted us to learn by our own mistakes. Sometimes that never happens. That is why there is so much suffering in this world. Many people want to blame it on God. Remember that Jesus never forced discipline on any of his disciples. That is why it took three years to be disciples and yet still some doubted. The only discipline that will help us is temperance. (Self-discipline). Self-control is the same as temperance which is one the fruits of the spirit.

[52] Christianity is based on self-discipline and Jesus did it by example. You cannot disciple

anyone without loving them. Our love for others is what makes others want to discipline themselves. The word 'disciple' comes from the word 'discipline'. The word discipline is not in the King James Bible but temperance is. Forced discipline is very destructive. Temperance is the key to the life of a Christian; it is only possible with love. That makes love the most important commandment.

[53] It is not easy to live under grace and we think it is much easier than living under law, yet so many under grace can't understand the difference between law and grace. We are under grace and not the law of the Old Testament. Grace is better but without love it is more difficult than keeping the law in the Old Testament. "Straight is the gate that leads to eternal life and few there be that find it.

[54] To be a good citizen is easy to think you are a good Christian. Under Grace we fail to see that suffering is needed. If we suffer with Christ we will reign with Him. And Jesus learned obedience by the things He suffered. Witnessing publicly, people tell me how hard it is to break a bad habit. They say; "I need to try harder" or "next time I will be stronger." But that doesn't happen; why? It is because of window shopping too long. A Christian must replace wrong thoughts with positive thoughts. When a temptation comes we need to immediately flee it. We must hate evil and love righteousness. Human nature wants to do both, for example; lustful thinking is wrong but because it is self-gratifying we will do it for a while and then go back to righteous living. That

is being double minded. James 1:8 "A doubled mined person is unstable in all his ways."

We can't serve two masters. We will either love the one and hate the other or cling to one and despise the other. We have the same problem in loving our enemies. We hate their sin and try to love them. We end up hating their sin along with the hate for them. We need to love the people that are sinners. So we need to separate their sin from the person.

[55] We nailed Jesus on the cross because of our sin. Jesus was willing to suffer for our sin. So suffering is an unwritten commandment of Christ but it falls under self-discipline. It takes suffering to separate ourselves from oursins and the sins of others.

When a church thinks that forced discipline is doing their job when in most cases it is only causing rebellion. If you discipline your children without love, you are doing more harm than good. If we do not suffer for our sin and the sin of others we will never understand Christ.

[56] With the government it is disobedience that forces the law to give you punishment. But a Christian with a wrong attitude will enforce discipline that will put a scar on the church that will ruin its' credibility.

[57] So the difference between government law and Christian law is the difference between the Old Testament and the New Testament. The Old Testament uses forced discipline and Grace is

under the New Testament which depends on self-discipline. This is why discipleship can't be controlled by preaching and teaching alone. There has to be daily mentoring along with much prayer. This is called discipleship. If there was any other way, Jesus would have used it when making disciples. We know with Jesus there is only one way but human nature looks for other ways constantly.

[58] Did Christ have any changes over the Sabbath Old Testament law? We know that the Ten Commandments is the only part of the Bible God wrote with his own finger. We must conclude what God writes with his own hand must be important for both the Old and New Testament, unless Jesus said differently.

[59] Jesus gave us no information how He was the Lord of the Sabbath and how the Sabbath was made for man and not man for the Sabbath but here is what we can conclude. In the Old Testament with about 1,500 regulations it is no doubt there was bondage. New regulations were unending and each one ignored, could have the death penalty. This is why the Jewish leaders wanted to find fault with Jesus concerning breaking the Sabbath laws. When Jesus had logical reasons for why it was permitted to pick corn on the Sabbath and why it was OK to heal on the Sabbath, the leaders were looking for another reason to condemn Jesus. They did so by using Jesus' own word making Himself equal with God, which they called blasphemy which was sufficient to condemn Jesus to death.

[60] Christ rose on the Sunday, so many think it is permissible to change the Sabbath from Saturday to Sunday. Better yet, since the priest were exempt from Sabbath day rules, because they were in service of the Lord. When Jesus said that He was the Lord of the Sabbath, everything He did was for the service of the Lord.

[61] Paul tells us also in Col 3:17 that all we do and say should be done for Christ. Acts 5:32 "The Holy Spirit is given to them that obey Him."

[62] Roman 10:17 Make sure your Scripture comes by the Holy Spirit. When churches use Scriptures that counterpoise one another it is not of the Holy Spirit. A fundamental church is when all churches have the same statements of faith.

[63] Statements of faith came about years ago to determine if you're a fundamental church or a cult. That is how the term, fundamental church, originated.

INDEX (reference between test numbers & Page numbers.)

This index is alsoa tie-in between text and Scriptures **Numbers in brackets are for paragraphs or sections references.**

PAGE 1

Ref. #   Scrip. Reference   Pg of Scripture

[1] [F]   Matthew 4:1-11   Pg40

[1] [E]	Matthew 4:14-16	Pg 41
[2] [E]	Matthew 4:14-17	Pg 42
[2]	Matthew 4:17-19	Pg 42
[2]	Matthew 10:5	Pg 47
[2]	Matthew 15:22-24	Pg 47

PAGE 2

Ref #	Scrip. Reference	Pg of Scripture
[6]	Romans 6:5	Pg 48
[7]	Acts 9:15	Pg 48

PAGE 3

Ref # Scripture Reference and scripture

[8] **Romans 6:17** *p3 #[8]* "¹⁷But God be thanked, that ye were the servants of sin, but ye have obeyed from the heart that form of doctrine which was delivered you."

[8] **Romans 16:17** "¹⁷Now I beseech you, brethren, mark them which cause divisions and offences contrary to the doctrine which ye have learned; and avoid them." P3 #[8]

[9] 1 Corinthians 13:3 see also p3

1 Corinthians 13:3 "³And though I bestow all my goods to feed *the poor*, and though I give my body to be burned, and have not charity, it profiteth me nothing." P3

[9] Romans 7:8-13; 13:16; 16:26 These Scriptures

Romans 7:8-13 "⁸But sin, taking occasion by the **commandment,** wrought in me all manner of concupiscence. For without the law sin *was* dead. [9]For I was alive without the law once: but when the **commandment** came, sin revived, and I died. [10]And the commandment, which *was ordained* to life, I found *to be* unto death. [11]For sin, taking occasion by the **commandment**, deceived me, and by it slew *me*. [12]Wherefore the law *is* holy, and the **commandment** holy, and just, and good. [13]Was then that which is good made death unto me? God forbid. But sin, that it might appear sin, working death in me by that which is good; that sin by the **commandment** might become exceeding sinful. ***Romans 13:9*** [9]For this, Thou shalt not commit adultery, Thou shalt not kill, Thou shalt not steal, Thou shalt not bear false witness, Thou shalt not covet; and if *there be* any other **commandment,** it is briefly comprehended in this saying, namely, Thou shalt love thy neighbour as thyself. ***Romans 16:26*** [26]But now is made manifest, and by the scriptures of the prophets, according to the **commandment** of the everlasting God, made known to all nations for the obedience of faith:"

PAGE 4

Ref.#	Reference	Pg of Scripture
[13]	Matthew 5:10-13; 5:21-23; 5:27-28; 5:38; 5 39:-41 5:43-44; 5:48	Pg 37 Matthew chap. 5 Matt 5:1-48

PAGE 5

[15] Revelation 18:4 "[4]"And I heard another voice from heaven, saying, Come out of her, my people, that ye be not partakers of her sins, and that ye receive not of her plagues."

PAGE 6

[17] Acts chapter 10 Scripture on Pg 44 Acts 10

[18] Acts 9:4 see Pg 50

[19] Acts chapter 10 Pg 44 [F] ACTS 10:1-48

PAGE 7

[24] Mark 2:27-28 Pg 17-18 under Mark 2:23-28

PAGE 8

[25] Romans 14 See p42 under Romans 14

PAGE 9

[29] Galatians 6:22-23 Scripture of Pg 50

[33] Matthew 4:11-22 Scripture on Pg 9

PAGE 14

[38] Matthew 6:14-15 "[14]For if ye forgive men their trespasses, your heavenly Father will also forgive you: [15]But if ye forgive not men their trespasses, neither will your Father forgive your trespasses."

Psalms 5:5 "[5]The foolish shall not stand in thy sight: thou hatest all workers of iniquity."

Matthew 5 Matthew 5:43-44 See Pg under Matt. Chapter 5

[39] **Matthew 12:1-2** p17 under Matt.12:1-13 p14 in text
Matt 12:1-2 "His diciples hungred and began to pluck the ears of corn to eat," v2 But the Pharisees saw it, they said unto Him, behold thy disciples do that which is not lawful to do upon the Sabbath Day.
[40] **Matthew 12:7** See Pg.17 Under Matt. 12:1-13 p14
Matt 12:7 "But if ye have known what this means, I will have mercy, and not sacrifice, ye would not have condemned the guiltless."

Page 15

[41] John 5:18 ***John 5:18*** "¹⁸Therefore the Jews sought the more to kill him, because he not only had broken the sabbath, but said also that God was his Father, making himself equal with God."
[42] ***Mark 14:62 through Mark 14:63*** ⁶²And Jesus said, I am: and ye shall see the Son of man sitting on the right hand of power, and coming in the clouds of heaven. ⁶³Then the high priest rent his clothes, and saith, What need we any further witnesses?
[43] ***Matthew 26:28*** ²⁸For this is my blood of the new testament, which is shed for many for the remission of sins.

[44] ***Matthew 26:66*** ⁶⁶What think ye? They answered and said, He is guilty of death.
[45] ***Mark 2:27-2:28*** ²⁷And he said unto them, The sabbath was made for man, and not man for the sabbath: ²⁸Therefore the Son of man is Lord also of the sabbath.

Page 16

[46] Romans 14:1-4 appendix #1 Pg. 42 Romans 14 p42-44

Page 17

APPENDIX # 1 large portions of Scriptures in order by the letters [A] to [D] p17
[A] New Testament Scripture on the Sabbath p17
[B] Old Testament Scripture on the Sabbath p24
[C] Matthew 5 first part to the Sermon on the Mount p37
[D] Matthew 4:1-20 p40
[E] Romans 14 p42
[F] Acts 10 p44

Page 47

APPENDIX #2 The paragaph number in brackets is on the left side of the Scripture references. Pg 47-50

1 John 2:15-16 See below:

1 John 2:15-16
[15]Love not the world, neither the things *that are* in the world. If any man love the world, the love of the Father is not in him. [16]For all that *is* in the world, the lust of the flesh, and the lust of the eyes, and the pride of life, is not of the Father, but is of the world.

Matthew 5:43-44 See below:

*Matthew **5:43-44***
[43]Ye have heard that it hath been said, Thou shalt love thy neighbour, and hate thine enemy. [44]But I say unto you, Love your enemies, bless them that curse you, do good to them that hate you, and pray for them which despitefully use you, and persecute you;

New testament Sabbath references of the Sabbath

Page 17
Matt 12:1-13

Matt 28:1

Mark 11:2

Mark 2:23-28

Page 19
Mark 3:2-4

Mark 15:42

Mark 16:1

Luke 4:16

Page 20
Luke 4:31

Luke 6:1-9

Page 21
Luke 13:10-16

Luke 14:1-5

Page 22
Luke 23:54-56

Matthew 12:1-13 The Pharisees accused Jesus of harvesting because He and His disciples plucked corn in the corn field. Jesus said, that David hungered and went into the house of God to eat the showbread on the Sabbath day which was not lawful. Jesus also said Priest profane on the Sabbath and are blameless.

Jesus also said the Son of God is Lord of the Sabbath.

Matthew 13:9 Jesus was in the Synagogue and the Pharisees said is it lawful to heal on the Sabbath. Jesus said if a sheep falls into a pit on the Sabbath will he not lift it out.

There was silence so Jesus healed the man with the withered hand.

Note: the other Gospels follow the same procedure as the Gospel of Matthew.

John 5:9-18

John 7:22-23

John 9:14-16

John 19:31

Phil 2:5-8

Old Testament Scriptures references of the Sabbath

Page 24
Ex 16:23-29

Ex 20:8-11

Page 25
Ex 31:13

Ex 31:14-16

Ex 35:2-3

Page 26

Lev 23:24

Lev 23:32

Page 27

Lev 23:39

Lev 25:1-8

Page 28
Lev 26:2

Scholars say that there are about 1,500 rules that give restrictions to what can be done on the Sabbath Day and breaking just one of them can be the death penalty.

There was always new rules being added to the Sabbath Day after the Law of Moses was written which are not found in the Old Testament but they were just as binding.

The early Christians changed the Sabbath Day from Saturday to Sunday, not that it was right. But Paul had the unwritten power to do so or it would have been stated by God's authority somewhere in the New Testament.

Num 15:32

Num 28-9-10

Deut 5:13-15

1 Chron 9:12

1 Chron 23:31

Page 29
2 Chron 2:4

2 Chron 8:13

2 Chron 23:4-8

Page 30:3
2 Chron 31:3

2 Chron 36:21

Neh 10:31

Neh 10:33

Page 31
Neh 13:15-19

Neh 13:22

Page 32
Isa 1:13

Isa 56:2-6

Christians take different positions on the rules of the Sabbath. Some are very strict in their rules and others ignore them altogether. I believe that both positions are Wong. When Jesus said that he was the Lord of the Sabbath He didn't say anything further but Paul did. So to ignore The Sabbath day is not correct. But to judge another man's opinion is not right either. It is basically left up to the individual. Remember the laws of our fathers kept the Sunday as the Holy Day to two respects Public stores were close and there was no professional sports on Sunday. These laws were in force for about 170 years. Hey are still laws because no law can be destroyed when it becomes statured law. But by **case law** they can be exceptions. So even our government has not eliminated the Day of Rest.

Remember to judge what someone

Else's rules will be sin. This is what seems to be the main problem today.

Isa 58:13

Page 33
Jer 17:21-27

Pg 34
Lam 1:7 Lam 2:6

Eze 20:12-13

Eze 20:11

Eze 20:11

Page 35
Eze 20:16

Eze 20:20

Eze 20:21

Eze 20:24

Eze 45:17

Eze 46:1-4

Eze 46:12

Amos 8:5

> In was very difficult in writing this book (lord of the Sabbath).
>
> The book has 66 pages but they are mostly Scriptures. I have only about 12 pages of my text. I didn't want to mixed my writings with the Scriptures so I decided to separate most of the Scriptures from my text and then by references tell where the Scriptures are found. To publish this book with so many references was difficult that I had to have several editions before the final publication.

Lord of the harvest - back cover with added information.

What did Jesus mean when He said that He was the Lord of the Sabbath? The Mosaic Law was of the Old Testament and most of the laws of the Old Testament came to an end. One of the exceptions are the 10 Commandments.

Jesus disagreed with the Jewish leaders when they tried to condemn Jesus for breaking two of the Sabbath day regulations concerning harvesting and healing. Jesus told the Jews where Grace stands concerning these two regulations and said that He was the Lord of the Sabbath. That showed that the dispensation of Grace was going to be different. Since Jesus gave Paul the Great Commission to the Gentiles, He also gave Paul the authority to change the Sabbath to be useful to man. Jesus said, that man was not made for the Sabbath but the Sabbath for man. In the Old Testament man was made to obey the 1,500 regulations which was bondage and just by breaking one regulation met death. Man was not made for the automobile but the automobile was made for man to serve him. The revision of the Sabbath Day is found in the book of Romans 14. The Sabbath day now was to be known as a holy day and it could be one day or every day depending on every man's decision. Paul said let a man be fully persuaded in this own mind. That goes also for what food to eat. The restriction is not to judge another if he was persuaded differently. Today I see most Christians going to both extremes. Some are going all out for the Sabbath and others forgetting all about honoring the Day of Rest as a holy day.

Made in the USA
Middletown, DE
10 October 2023

40580045R00038